MEDIEVAL ENGLAND

To Sue, Roger, Nolan, and Nathaniel

The author wishes to specially thank
Professor Catherine McKenna, Coordinator of Medieval Studies
at the Graduate Center of the City University of New York
for her invaluable help in reading the manuscript.

CULTURES OF THE PAST

MEDIEVAL ENGLAND

KATHRYN HINDS

BENCHMARK BOOKS

MARSHALL CAVENDISH
NEW YORK

Benchmark Books
Marshall Cavendish Corporation
99 White Plains Road
Tarrytown, New York 10591-9001

Website: www.marshallcavendish.com

© Marshall Cavendish Corporation 2002

Library of Congress Cataloging-in-Publication Data

Hinds, Kathryn, 1962-
    Medieval England / by Kathryn Hinds.
        p. cm. — (Cultures of the past)
    Includes bibliographical references and index.
    ISBN 0-7614-0308-6 (lib. bdg.)
        1. Great Britain—History—Medieval period, 1066–1485—Juvenile literature. 2. England—Civilization—1066-1485—Juvenile literature. [1. Great Britain—History—Medieval period, 1066-1485. 2. England—Civilization—1066-1485.] I. Title. II. Series.
    DA175 .H555   2001
    942.03—dc21   00-046769

Printed in Hong Kong

1 3 5 6 4 2

Book design by Carol Matsuyama
Photo research by Rose Corbett Gordon, Mystic CT

Front cover: Chaucer's Canterbury pilgrims, from a fourteenth-century manuscript.

Back cover: A nobleman, his hunting hawk perched on his wrist, with an escort of warriors. From the eleventh-century Bayeux Tapestry.

Photo Credits

Front cover: courtesy of The Art Archive/British Library; back cover: courtesy of The Art Archive/Musée de la Tapisserie Bayeux/Dagli Orti; pages 3, 37, 41, 52, 59: British Library, London, UK/Bridgeman Art Library; page 7: Private Collection/Bridgeman Art Library; pages 9, 39: The Pierpont Morgan Library/Art Resource, NY; pages 10, 32: Ted Spiegel/The Image Works; page 11: The Art Archive/Musée de la Tapisserie Bayeux/Dagli Orti; pages 12, 20, 33: Erich Lessing/Art Resource; page 13: The Art Archive/British Museum; page 16: The Art Archive/JFB; pages 17, 66: Bettmann/CORBIS; pages 22-23: Topham/The Image Works; page 24: Art Resource, NY; page 25: Michelle Garrett/CORBIS; page 29: Mary Evans Picture Library/British Museum; page 30: Northwind Pictures; page 35: Biblioteca Nazionale, Turin, Italy/Roger-Viollet, Paris/Bridgeman Art Library; pages 43, 53: The Art Archive/British Library; page 45: The Art Archive/Victoria and Albert Museum London/Graham Brandon; page 47: Mary Evans Picture Library/Laurence B. Saint; page 49: CORBIS/Archivo Iconografico, S.A.; page 50: Mary Evans Picture Library/Stephen Reid; pages 55, 70: The Art Archive/British Library; pages 61, 64: CORBIS/Adam Woolfitt; page 62: The Art Archive/Honourable Soc of Inner Temple/Eileen Tweedy; page 63: The Art Archive; page 65: Bill Lai/The Image Works; page 67: Mary Evans Picture Library/N.C. Wyeth.

ACKNOWLEDGMENT

Quotes from William FitzStephen's description of London, pp. 28–29, from Elizabeth Hallam, *The Plantagenet Chronicles*, pp. 98, 100–101. Translation of selection from Geoffrey Chaucer, *The Canterbury Tales*, p. 37, by Kathryn Hinds. Quote from Ralph of Diceto, p. 41, from Elizabeth Hallam, *The Plantagenet Chronicles*, p. 208. Adaptations from Geoffrey Chaucer, *The Canterbury Tales*, p. 55, by Kathryn Hinds. All biblical quotations are from the Holy Bible, Revised Standard Version.

CONTENTS

CHAPTER ONE

KINGS, QUEENS, AND CONFLICT

England is a small country located on the island of Britain just off the west coast of the continent of Europe. In spite of its size, it has been one of the most powerful and influential nations on earth for many centuries. It has played major roles in world politics, the arts, society, and religion. The roots of England's strength and distinction can be found in the historical period we know as the Middle Ages, the years from roughly 500 to 1500.

The Coming of the English

In early times most of Britain was inhabited by many tribes of people called Britons. The northern part of the island was occupied by the Picts, about whom little is known today. In the year 43, Britain was invaded by the Roman Empire. Soon Rome controlled all of the island except for the Pictish lands. Britain was part of the Roman Empire for hundreds of years, but Britons still made up the majority of the island's population. In 410 the empire granted independence to Britain. Without the protection of Rome's military might, the Britons were now open to attack. Raiders swept down from the Pictish lands and across the sea from Ireland with increasing frequency and violence.

Around the middle of the fifth century, British rulers hired mercenaries, foreign warriors, to help fight the raiders. These mercenaries, usually known as Anglo-Saxons, came from what are now Denmark and Germany.

The mercenaries were given land in southeastern Britain. But soon the Anglo-Saxons rebelled and established their own kingdom, Kent. More and more Anglo-Saxons came to settle in Britain. Sometimes the settlement was peaceful, but often it was not. The Britons fought back as well as they could. In the late fifth century, they were able to drive back the Anglo-Saxons for a time; according to legend, this was the doing of King Arthur.

King Offa of Mercia (757–796) was the first ruler to proclaim himself "king of all the English." From his kingdom of Mercia in central England, he was able to extend his power throughout the southern part of the country.

During the next hundred years, Anglo-Saxons gained control of three-fifths of the island. Eventually the Britons held only the west and north, the countries that came to be known as Wales and Scotland. The rest of Britain was now Angle Land: England.

Anglo-Saxons and Vikings

By the year 700, there were seven Anglo-Saxon kingdoms. The most powerful of these were Northumbria in the north, Mercia in central

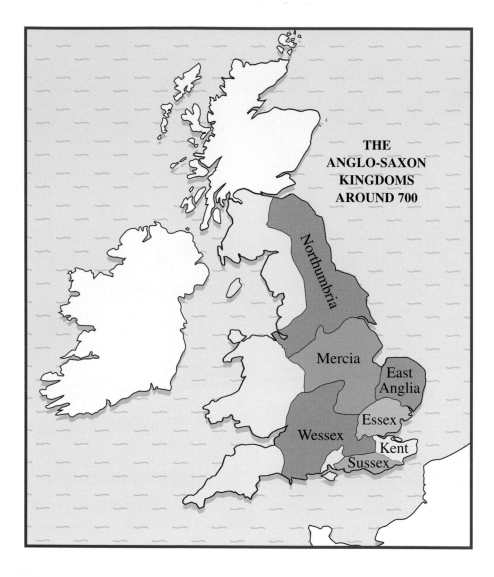

THE ANGLO-SAXON KINGDOMS AROUND 700

Northumbria

Mercia

East Anglia

Essex

Wessex

Kent

Sussex

England, and Wessex in the southwest. Wars had been frequent as the kingdoms vied with one another for power. But even in their separate kingdoms, the Anglo-Saxons were starting to think of themselves as one people, the English. In 802 the rulers of Wessex began claiming the title "king of the English." The Wessex kings did bring most of southern England under their rule, but before long they had serious competition for control of the island.

Vikings, seaborne warriors from Scandinavia, had raided a wealthy monastery on the coast of Northumbria in 793. This was the first of many

Viking attacks on Britain. In 866 a large Viking force landed in England. The Vikings swiftly conquered Northumbria, followed later by East Anglia and Mercia. Only Wessex was able to resist the invasion, thanks to the leadership of Alfred the Great, king of Wessex.

In 886 Alfred made a treaty with the Vikings that gave them territory in northeastern England. In this area, which came to be known as the Danelaw, the raiders and their families settled down to farm and do business. They founded the Kingdom of York, with the thriving city of York at its center.

Alfred united the rest of England under his own rule. He built many new, strongly fortified towns in strategic places. Alfred also promoted education, literature, history, and religion.

In 902 Alfred the Great's son and successor, Edward, began to reconquer the Danelaw. In 917 he and his sister Aethelflaed, Lady of the Mercians, decisively defeated the Vikings, winning back to England all but the Kingdom of York. York remained under Viking rule until 954.

The Viking force known as the Great Army invades England in 866. The army's leader, Ingvar the Boneless, became the first Viking ruler of York.

But the Vikings were not yet done with England. Their raids soon resumed with fierce intensity. Then, in 1013, the Danish king Svein Forkbeard conquered the country. In 1016 his son Canute took the English throne. Canute also ruled Denmark and much of Norway, but he lived most of his life in England. His rule was firm but fair, and England was at peace throughout his reign.

Many of the Vikings who settled down on farms in England lived in longhouses like this one in northern Scotland's Shetland Islands.

Conquest!

The English crown returned to Anglo-Saxon hands with the rule of Edward the Confessor, the great-great-great-grandson of Alfred the Great. Edward was a deeply religious man who was responsible for the building of Westminster Abbey, a famous church near London. He had no children, so he chose his wife's brother Harold Godwinson to succeed him.

Harold became king in January 1066, and within months was forced to fight for his throne. First he defeated a challenge from his brother, then fought off a Norwegian invasion. Almost immediately he faced another enemy, William, duke of Normandy. A cousin of Edward the Confessor, William claimed that the English crown had been promised to him. In the fall of 1066, he sailed from his lands in northern France, taking with him a large, well-trained army.

Because they came from Normandy, William and his followers (and, later, their descendants) were called Normans. At the Battle of Hastings, on October 14, 1066, the Normans defeated the English army led by Harold, who was killed in battle. After two more months of hard fighting, William marched into London, and on Christmas Day he was crowned king of England.

William the Conqueror, as he became known, did everything he could to strengthen royal power in England. He confiscated almost all of the English nobles' lands, keeping some under his personal control and distributing most of the rest to his Norman followers. He then required all landholders to swear loyalty to him. In 1086 he ordered a national census—England's first—so that he could calculate the services and taxes that the landholders owed him. The record of this survey was called the Domesday Book; it still exists, and it has given historians much information about medieval England.

A scene from the Battle of Hastings, from the Bayeux Tapestry. The tapestry, a 230-foot-long strip of linen, is embroidered with many images of William of Normandy's conquest of England. People used to think that it might have been made by William's wife, Matilda, but many scholars now believe that it was created by Englishwomen.

A Family of Kings

William the Conqueror was succeeded by two of his sons, first William II (William Rufus), and then Henry I. Henry I's only son died in a shipwreck, so he named his daughter Matilda as his successor.

After Henry I's death, however, his nephew Stephen came from France and seized the throne. This action began a civil war between Stephen's and Matilda's followers, which lasted for most of Stephen's reign. Finally the king ended the conflict by agreeing that his heir would be Matilda's son, Henry, who became Henry II.

Henry's kingdom was practically an empire. Not only did he rule England, but he and his French wife, Eleanor of Aquitaine, together held more French territory than the king of France himself. This caused a great deal of conflict between Henry and the French king. Henry split his time between England and France, seeing to his interests and defending his lands in both countries. He also became the first English king to claim lordship over Wales, Scotland, and Ireland, although he did not try to conquer these neighboring countries. During most of Henry's rule, England was peaceful and prosperous, but the end of his reign was troubled with rebellions by his ambitious sons.

Henry was succeeded by his son Richard I. Known as Richard the

Eleanor of Aquitaine made Henry II's court a center of music, poetry, and other arts. The artist who created this sculpture for Eleanor's tomb portrayed her as if she had just fallen asleep while reading, so that she would always be remembered for her great love of learning and literature.

Richard I (left) in battle against Saladin, the sultan of Egypt and Syria, during the Third Crusade. The two leaders eventually negotiated a treaty that allowed European Christians to make peaceful pilgrimages to Jerusalem, but Saladin kept control of the holy city.

Lionheart, today he is one of the most famous kings of England. He was a brave and enthusiastic warrior who played a leading role in the Third Crusade. This was one of a series of wars, the Crusades, that European Christians fought in the Middle East to gain and keep control of the land where Jesus had lived.

On Richard's way home from the war, he was captured by the duke of Austria and held for ransom for two years. After his release, he spent nearly all the rest of his reign fighting to hold his lands in France, the country where he had spent most of his life. During Richard's absences, England was governed by various royal officials and by his mother, Queen Eleanor.

While Richard ruled, the people of England had to pay heavy taxes to support his wars and pay his ransom. When he was succeeded by his brother John, the situation grew even worse. John increased the people's tax burden and imposed England's first income tax. For much of his reign, he was at war with the king of France. King John not only lost this conflict, but he lost all of the French lands he had inherited, breaking a connection between England and France that had existed since the Norman Conquest.

John also broke with the past by ignoring the customs surrounding the relationship between the king and his barons, or chief nobles. Among other offenses, he demanded more military service from them than previous kings had and he refused to consult with them about new taxes and the like. The barons rebelled against John, and in 1215 they forced him to sign Magna Carta, a groundbreaking charter in which the king promised to uphold the barons' traditional rights.

English Expansion

John's son and successor, Henry III, tried to win back the French lands once held by his family, without success. Henry's son, Edward I, had other ideas about expanding England's rule. In 1284 he conquered Wales and placed Welsh lands under the control of English nobles. He invaded Scotland in 1296. The Scots rebelled against English rule, led first by William Wallace and later by Robert Bruce. Edward died while he was leading an army north to subdue Bruce.

Edward I's reign was disastrous for Wales and Scotland. However, England not only gained new territory, but also saw the beginnings of a new system of government. Like his father, Edward had a parliament, a council of advisers drawn from among the barons and church leaders. During the course of his wars, Edward enlarged his council and called it together more frequently. In 1295 he held the Model Parliament and set the pattern for future meetings of Parliament, which would become the lawmaking branch of England's government.

Edward's son, Edward II, continued the war to hold Scotland. But at the Battle of Bannockburn in 1314, Robert Bruce decisively defeated the English. Edward II's military failures, combined with his corrupt policies and unpleasant personality, made him one of England's most disliked kings. His own wife, Isabella, led a rebellion against him. With the support of most of the barons, she forced Edward to pass the crown on to his son, who reigned as Edward III. This king earned a reputation as an ideal ruler and warrior.

A Turbulent Century

Edward III claimed to be France's rightful ruler, since his mother was the sister of the king of France, who had died without a son to succeed him.

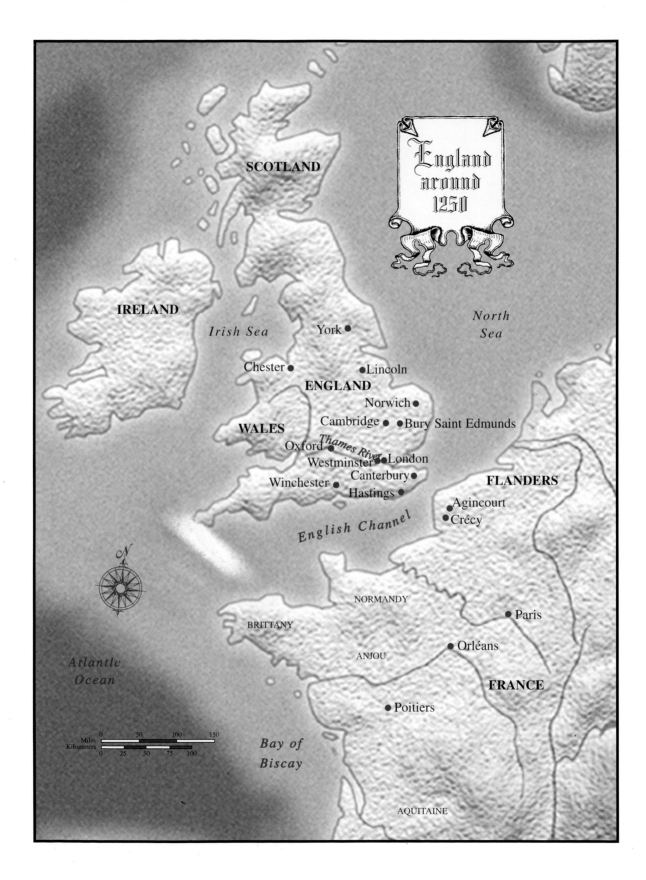

England around 1250

SCOTLAND

IRELAND

Irish Sea

York •

Chester •

North Sea

ENGLAND

Lincoln •

Norwich •

WALES

Cambridge • • Bury Saint Edmunds

Oxford • *Thames River*

Westminster • • London

Winchester • Canterbury •

Hastings •

English Channel

FLANDERS

Agincourt •
• Crécy

N

NORMANDY

BRITTANY

• Paris

ANJOU

• Orléans

Atlantic Ocean

FRANCE

• Poitiers

Miles
Kilometers

0   50   100   150
0 25 50 75 100

Bay of Biscay

AQUITAINE

English forces attacking a French castle during the Hundred Years War. The English are shown with two cannons, which used an explosion of gunpowder to fire iron shot. These recently invented weapons were powerful, but not as accurate or reliable as arrows fired by expert archers.

To win the French crown, in 1337 Edward launched a war that was to go down in history as the Hundred Years War. The battles were all fought in France, and the English army was often hugely outnumbered. Nevertheless, during Edward's reign the English won two major battles, at Crécy (kray-SEE) and Poitiers (pwah-TYAY). The great hero of both battles was the king's son Edward, called the Black Prince because of the color of his armor.

In spite of these English victories, things were not well at home. In the early 1300s, there had been a great famine, and at least half a million people starved to death. This was followed by epidemics of typhoid fever and livestock diseases. Then, in 1348–1349, a terrible plague known as the Black Death swept through England, killing 50,000 people in London alone. The nation as a whole lost more than half its population.

The war with France dragged on. King Richard II, the Black Prince's son, imposed heavy taxes to help pay for the war. He also demanded forced labor from the peasants and took away many of their traditional rights. The result was a peasants' rebellion in 1381. A blacksmith named Wat Tyler led thousands of peasants in a march on London. They confronted the king, who promised to meet many of their demands. However, Tyler was killed, royal forces crushed the rebellion, and the king kept none of his promises.

Richard II was as unpopular with the barons as he was with the peasants. In 1399 his cousin Henry Bolingbroke, duke of Lancaster, led a

Victims of the Black Death. There was no cure for this highly contagious disease, and nearly everyone who came down with it died, usually within four days.

revolt against him. Richard was removed from the throne, and Parliament gave the kingship to Bolingbroke, who ruled as Henry IV. His reign was continually threatened by rebellious plots among powerful nobles. One of Henry IV's greatest enemies was the Welsh patriot Owain Glyn Dŵr (Owen Glendower), who led a revolution that nearly freed Wales from English rule.

SCENES FROM ROYAL LIFE

By the fifteenth century, the king of England was surrounded by a great deal of luxury and ceremony. He had a number of castles and palaces where he held court. In each of these royal residences, the king's chamber was partitioned into three rooms. The outermost was the audience chamber, where he greeted ambassadors and the like. Then there was an inner room, the privy chamber, where he could hold private conferences. Beyond that lay the bedchamber. However, the king had little privacy even here. Attendants known as Squires for the Body helped him dress and undress, and at night they slept on the floor near his bed.

The king had numerous other attendants, courtiers with specific duties and grand-sounding titles. At meals, for example, twenty Squires for the Household waited on the king. Dishes were presented one at a time and with great ceremony, supervised by a Server. An attendant called a Ewer (YOO-er) stood by with a washbasin and towel so that the king could clean up between courses. A royal physician was also present, to advise the king on the healthfulness of his diet. All during meals, thirteen minstrels were required to play music to entertain the king and help him digest his food.

Even bedtime was a grandiose affair. With two Squires for the Body standing by the head of the bed and two Grooms of the Chamber by the foot, Yeomen of the Chamber brought in the bedding. A Gentleman Usher held back the bed's heavy curtain while the sheets and blankets were laid down. The pillows were plumped up, the covers were folded down exactly forty-five inches, and holy water was sprinkled over all. Only then could the king finally go to bed, resting up for another day of government and ceremony.

Henry IV was followed on the throne by his son Henry, a skilled leader and warrior. Henry V stepped up the war with France and personally led an army to try to take the French crown. Thanks to the skill of his archers, he won a crushing victory at the Battle of Agincourt (A-jun-kort) in 1415. He went on to conquer all of northern France. He married the king's daughter and forced the king to declare him heir to the French throne.

Henry V was succeeded by his baby son, Henry VI, and England began to lose ground in France. In 1429 Joan of Arc, a young peasant woman, led the French army to victory in the Battle of Orléans. The English suffered further defeats, and by the war's end in 1453, they were left holding only one city on France's northern coast.

The White Rose and the Red

As a grown man, Henry VI was kind and religious, but he was a weak and unpopular king. Richard, duke of York, a descendant of Edward III, claimed that he had a better right to rule than Henry. A long series of wars broke out between Richard's supporters, the Yorkists, and Henry's supporters, the Lancastrians (who got their name because Henry's grandfather had been the duke of Lancaster). Since the symbol of the house of York was a white rose and the symbol of the house of Lancaster a red rose, the conflict became known as the Wars of the Roses.

Richard, duke of York, was killed early on, but in 1461 his son Edward won the crown from Henry VI, who won it back nine years later. The next year Edward, who ruled as Edward IV, defeated Henry once and for all.

At Edward's death in 1483, his twelve-year-old son became king. Because of the king's youth, Edward's brother Richard governed England as Protector of the Realm. Richard soon had to crush a plot by the young king's mother's family to seize power. After this, Parliament declared Richard king, and he was crowned as Richard III. The boy-king and his younger brother were sent to the Tower of London; they were never seen again, and to this day no one knows for certain what happened to them.

Richard had enemies among both the Yorkists and the Lancastrians. These enemies helped Henry Tudor, who claimed the crown as a descendant of the Lancastrian kings, return from exile in France and invade England. In 1485 Richard III was killed in the Battle of Bosworth Field,

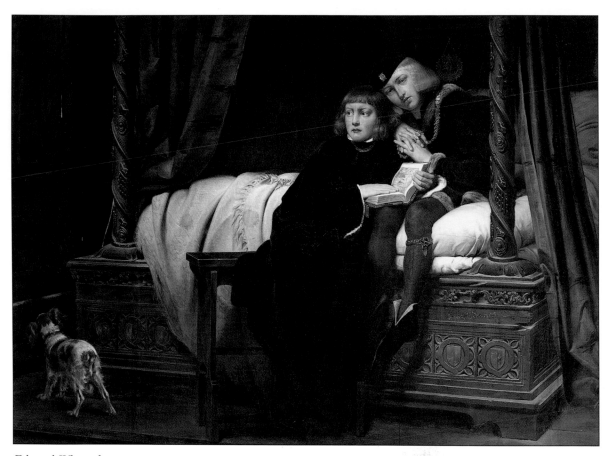

Edward IV's unhappy sons are shown confined in the Tower of London in this 1830 painting by Paul Delaroche. Some writers, including Shakespeare, believed that the boys were later murdered by Richard III, but modern historians cannot find any proof of the children's fate.

and Henry's army was victorious. Henry Tudor took the throne as King Henry VII. He then married Edward IV's daughter, uniting the houses of Lancaster and York and bringing peace to the land with a new dynasty, the Tudors.

~<

By the end of the fifteenth century, great changes were happening all over Europe. Among scholars and writers, there had been growing interest in the philosophy and literature of ancient Greece and Rome. Based on these ancient sources, new ideas were starting to affect the way people approached the arts, government, and religion. In the 1450s Johannes Gutenberg of Germany had invented the printing press; William Caxton set up

NEW WORLD, NEW AGE

Henry VII was king of England when Europe's Age of Exploration was in full swing. Like many other European rulers, Henry was eager to find new trade routes and new markets for his country's goods. In 1496 he gave John Cabot permission to sail to the New World on behalf of England.

Cabot, an Italian mapmaker and merchant, had moved to England in the 1480s. After Columbus's voyage, Cabot thought that he could find a better route by crossing the Atlantic farther north. At this time people still believed that Columbus had reached Asia, which had supplied Europe with spices, jewels, and other luxuries for centuries.

Cabot set sail in May 1497. On June 24 he landed in what is now Canada, somewhere between Nova Scotia and Newfoundland. Believing he had reached Asia, he returned in triumph to England. He had not brought back any treasure, but he had discovered the rich Atlantic fishing grounds known as the Grand Banks.

In 1508, toward the end of Henry VII's reign, Cabot's son Sebastian also made a voyage to North America for England. By this time Europeans realized that Columbus and John Cabot had not reached Asia but another continent entirely. Sebastian Cabot was looking for the Northwest Passage, a waterway that would cut through this continent so that sailors could reach Asia. Instead he found Hudson Bay in Canada. He also sailed south and explored some of the North American coast before returning to England.

Both Cabots claimed North American lands for England. A century later, these claims would give England the basis for establishing its New World colonies. In the meantime, the Cabots' voyages gave England a wider view of itself, its role in the world, and its potential for achievement. The English were leaving the Middles Ages behind and moving into a new age.

England's first printing press in London in 1476. The growing availability of mass-produced books contributed greatly to the exchange of new ideas of all kinds. Soon reformers would challenge the power of the Catholic Church, shattering the religious unity that had been a major part of medieval European culture. In 1534 Henry VII's heir, Henry VIII, would found the Church of England, with himself at its head, leaving the Middle Ages behind once and for all.

CHAPTER TWO

ENGLAND'S GREEN AND PLEASANT LAND

In the Middle Ages, the majority of the English people lived in the countryside and were involved with farming or processing farm products. Peasant farmers raised most of the food eaten by the nation's people. Many farms were devoted to raising sheep, and English wool was famous

for its quality all over Europe. English merchants made a big business out of exporting it. Much wool stayed at home, though. From the thirteenth century on, the production of woolen cloth was one of England's major industries. Such enterprises spurred the growth of cities as centers of trade, manufacturing, banking, and education.

Cities were also becoming centers of government administration. The power to govern was linked with military might, though. This gave great importance to castles, which dominated many cities, river crossings, border areas, and other strategic locations. These fortresses were symbols of one kind of power; churches were symbols of another. The influence of the Christian

An artist's reconstruction of fifteenth-century Wharram Percy in northern England. Villages like this were home to most of medieval England's population.

religion in the Middle Ages, described more fully in the next chapter, could be felt almost everywhere. Today we see the visible remains of this age of faith: awe-inspiring churches and beautiful religious books, written and illustrated by hand, that have survived the centuries. Writers and artists created many other kinds of books, too, producing a body of literature that reflects the range and richness of medieval English culture.

Country Places

A typical English village in the Middle Ages had between thirty and forty houses. Each house had a yard, enclosed by a ditch or fence, where storage sheds, animal pens, and other outbuildings might be located. Behind most houses there was also a garden of about half an acre, where the family raised its vegetables and perhaps grew fruit trees.

A typical scene of medieval English peasant life: farm workers milking sheep and carrying the milk away for processing.

Village houses ranged from tiny one-room cottages to high-ceilinged longhouses divided into four or five sections. In a longhouse one end of the building might be partitioned off as a storeroom, while at the other end there could be an attached byre, or barn, to house livestock. In this way the animals were sheltered from bad weather, and in the winter their body heat helped keep the human residents of the house warm.

Peasant houses were often built of wattle and daub. In this construction method, the wall consisted of a framework of vertical posts with flexible sticks woven between them—the wattle. This was filled in and plastered on both sides with a mixture of mud and straw—the daub. The roof was usually thatched with straw, and the floors were of hard-packed earth. Many such houses did not stand the test of time: a village family generally had to rebuild its home every forty or so years.

Most English villages included a manor house, owned by the knight or baron who held the village land. This large stone building stood on an acre or two of ground and was often surrounded by a wall, fence, or moat. The most important feature of the manor house was the great hall, a huge, high-ceilinged room

A manor house surrounded by a moat. Thousands of moated manor houses were built in England during the thirteenth century. The moats were not only for security but were also status symbols.

where guests were entertained, holidays celebrated, and meetings held. Other village buildings might include one or more mills, where grain was ground into flour; ovens or bake houses; a forge, where a blacksmith made horseshoes and iron tools; and the village church.

The village center was surrounded by fields, where crops such as grain, peas, and beans were grown. Usually the village farmland was divided into three large fields. Every year one field was left fallow, one was planted in the fall, and one was planted in the spring. Cattle, sheep, and horses were allowed to graze in the fields after the crops were harvested.

Crowded Cities

Throughout the Middle Ages, all over Europe, cities grew in size and importance. England's greatest city was London. Like most medieval towns, London was protected by tall, thick stone walls. They had been built in Roman times and were strengthened during the Middle Ages. People entered and left a city through gates in the wall. Various buildings clustered outside city gates: taverns and inns, small monasteries, kennels for hunting dogs, fishermen's huts, and the like. Many medieval cities had close ties with the countryside and were surrounded by fields, orchards, and gardens, which some townspeople went out to tend every day. Wealthy city dwellers sometimes built mansions in these neighboring rural areas.

Within the city walls, streets were crowded with pedestrians, horses, and carts. Cats, dogs, geese, chickens, pigs, sheep, and cattle were also liable to be in the street. Medieval city streets were generally narrow, unpaved, muddy, and smelly. At many places the streets opened out onto large squares, places where people could gather for celebrations or everyday socializing. Fairs and markets were held in the squares, too. Outside these open squares, buildings tended to crowd together.

In general, townspeople made their home their place of business as well. An independent craftsperson would have a shop and workshop on the ground floor of a house, and the family would live on the upper floors. Well-to-do merchants often had a good-sized piece of land, with a yard and garden around their homes. A merchant's house would have a showroom for merchandise and an office for keeping accounts, as well as fairly spacious living quarters for the family. But in poorer neighborhoods several families lived in each house, renting their rooms from the house's owner. A very poor family might have only one room.

Even for the wealthy, cleanliness was a challenge in the medieval city. Water for drinking, cooking, and washing had to be carried from a well outside the house; often many houses shared a single well. People generally bathed once a week at most. Fleas, bedbugs, and lice were constant problems. To go to the bathroom, most people had to use an outhouse in the yard. Some homes might have a garderobe, a kind of indoor outhouse, off the bedroom. Garderobes often emptied into nearby canals, streams, or ditches, contributing to the city's smelly and unhealthy atmosphere.

Power Centers

Although most people lived in country villages and a growing number lived in cities, today when we think of medieval England, we tend to think mainly of castles and their residents. Indeed, castles are among the most impressive and lasting remains of this time in history.

When William the Conqueror invaded England in 1066, he brought with him an enthusiasm for castle building. In 1066 there were only half a dozen castles in England; by 1100 there were five hundred. The earliest type of castle was usually a tall, wooden, rectangular tower, called a keep, surrounded by a timber fence on top of a huge earthen mound.

Stone castles began to be built during the twelfth century. These strongholds were protected by high, thick walls with towers at their corners and at points along their length. Edward I, who brought English castle building to a peak in the thirteenth century, often had castles built with two walls, one surrounding the other.

At the simplest castles, a keep was the major building, with a storage area on the ground floor, a great hall above it, and living quarters on the top floor. The walls of more elaborate castles enclosed a number of buildings and facilities. The largest structure was the great hall, where the castle's lord held court. The castle's residents also ate their meals together in the great hall. And early on, everyone in the castle slept in the great hall. The lord and his wife had some privacy behind a partition at one end of the building. Later, the lord and lady's chamber was often a room above the hall or on an upper floor of one of the castle towers.

Because of the castle's military function, within the walls there were

MEDIEVAL LONDON

In the 1170s William FitzStephen wrote a biography of Saint Thomas à Becket. The saint was born and raised in London, and so his biographer devoted part of his book to a description of that city. From FitzStephen we learn that twelfth-century London had three castles and 139 churches. About two miles west of the city, at Westminster, was the king's palace, "a building incomparable in its ramparts and bulwarks."

"A populous suburb" lay between Westminster and London. Around the suburban houses were "spacious and beautiful gardens . . . planted with trees." North of London, streams ran through "pastures and pleasant meadow lands," and nearby were fertile grainfields and forests full of wild animals.

Medieval London, on the banks of the Thames River, was a major center of international trade. FitzStephen wrote that "from every nation under heaven merchants delight to bring their trade by sea." From the Middle East came gold, spices, incense, palm oil, and precious gems. Silk came from China. Merchants from Scandinavia and Russia brought furs, while French merchants sold wine.

Wineshops clustered along the riverbank. In this same neighborhood, there was also a "public cook-shop," a kind of take-out restaurant. This convenience greatly impressed FitzStephen, who described it enthusiastically: "There daily you may find food according to the season, dishes of meat, roast, fried and boiled, large and small fish, coarser meats for the poor and more delicate for the rich. . . . However great the multitude of soldiers and travellers entering the city . . . at any hour of the day or night . . . they turn aside thither, if they please, where every man can refresh himself in his own way."

FitzStephen also wrote about the ways some Londoners celebrated holidays. On summer feast days young men enjoyed sports—"archery, running, jumping, wrestling, slinging the stone, hurling the javelin beyond a mark and fighting with a sword and [small shield]"—while young women preferred to dance until the moon rose. For winter holidays, men hunted wild boars and other game animals to provide meat for festive meals. Sometimes a marsh north of the city froze over, and young men went there "to play games on the ice." Some had fun simply sliding over the

London around the year 1500. London Bridge can be seen in the background, with some of the city's many church spires rising behind it. In the foreground is the Tower of London, the royal castle that William the Conqueror began building in 1078.

frozen marsh. Others, "more skilled at winter sports," enjoyed a cross between ice-skating and skiing: they "put on their feet the shin-bones of animals, binding them firmly round their ankles, and holding poles shod with iron in their hands, which they strike from time to time against the ice, they are propelled swift as a bird in flight."

All in all, FitzStephen thought very highly of the city of London: "I do not think there is a city with a better record for church-going, doing honour to God's ordinances. . . , celebrating weddings, providing feasts, entertaining guests, and also, it may be added, in care for funerals and for the burial of the dead. The only plagues of London are the immoderate drinking of fools and the frequency of fires."

To strengthen his hold on England, William the Conqueror ordered the building of Nottingham Castle, in the north, in 1067. This is how the castle looked in the 1500s. It was destroyed during warfare a century later.

usually barracks for soldiers. Near the barracks would be a stable for the knights' warhorses, and for saddle horses and packhorses. A blacksmith worked at a forge close by, making horseshoes and other necessities.

Other animals within the castle walls included cats, which protected stored food from mice and rats, and hunting hounds. A lord's favorite dogs might follow him wherever he went in the castle, and many ladies had pet lapdogs.

Houses of God

In village, town, or castle, there was always a place set aside for religion. In many villages the church was the only building constructed of stone. Every castle had at least one chapel, which might be just a small chamber tucked into a tower or a room as big as a regular church. Cities had numerous churches—by the year 1200, there were about 140 in London.

Some of England's most splendid churches were built or

COMPARING THE COMFORTS OF HOME

Even for the rich and powerful, comforts were limited in the Middle Ages. Things most of us take for granted today—central heating, indoor plumbing, electric lights—simply did not exist. Comforts did improve over time: In the twelfth century, fireplaces, newly invented, began to replace open hearths as a heat source. The fourteenth century saw the first European use of rugs, which made floors warmer. The same period introduced tapestries, elaborately woven wall hangings, which were not only beautiful but also helped cut down on drafts. Such improvements were available mainly to the wealthy—for whom life was still not entirely comfortable. Fleas, lice, and bedbugs infested all medieval dwellings, from peasant cottage to royal castle. People generally bathed only once a week, if that, and clothes were not washed often, either. Privacy, even in a castle or great manor house, was almost unknown. The table below gives some idea of how comfortable a person could expect to be at home in village, town, or castle.

	Village	Town	Castle
Floor	dirt, strewn with rushes usually	wood, with rushes or rug	wood or stone, with rushes or rug
Windows	few, small; shutters but sometimes no other covering	covered with oiled parchment or wax-coated cloth	few and very narrow on lower levels; some large and with glass on upper floors
Heat	open hearth	fireplace	fireplace
Light	hearth, oil lamps, occasionally tallow candles	fireplace, oil lamps, candles (tallow and occasionally beeswax)	fireplace, oil lamps, candles (tallow and beeswax)
Water Supply	village well, nearby streams, et cetera	neighborhood well, nearby river, et cetera	well, cisterns
Bathing	barrel full of water	public bathhouse, sometimes wooden bathtub at home	wooden bathtub in bedroom as needed, occasionally permanent bathhouse
Sanitation	trench in yard, or any spot "a bow shot away" from the house	outhouse in yard, sometimes garderobe in bedroom	garderobes
Beds	straw-filled mattresses	straw-filled mattresses (for the poor) or large canopied beds (for the rich)	straw-filled mattresses or trundle beds (for servants), large canopied beds (for nobles)

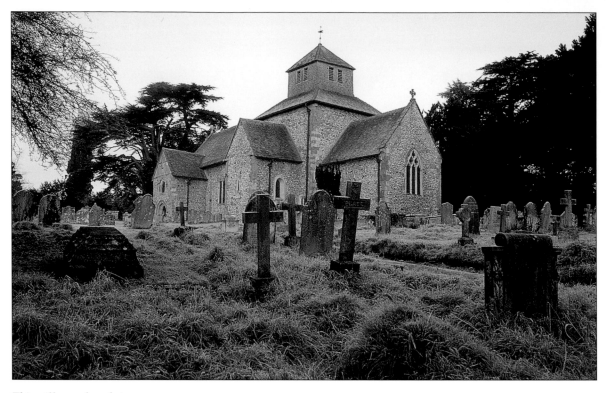

This village church in southern England was built around the year 1000. It is one of the most complete Anglo-Saxon churches still standing.

renovated during the twelfth through fourteenth centuries. Builders used a new style of architecture that became popular in the 1100s. This style, employed in churches throughout western Europe, was later named Gothic architecture. It was marked by soaring stone structures and tall, pointed arches, which drew worshippers' eyes toward heaven.

Gothic churches featured large windows set into their high walls. Colored glass was easier to produce at this time than clear glass, so church designers created stained glass windows. With pictures made of colored glass, artists illustrated episodes from the Bible and other religious scenes. Many worshippers could not read or understand most of the church service (which was in Latin), and for these people, church windows provided a visual version of the Bible.

Churches were also adorned with sculptures of religious scenes, saints, kings and queens, and imaginary creatures. Other kinds of artwork filled houses of worship, too. Choir stalls, where priests and their helpers sat during services, often featured elaborate wood carvings. The candlesticks and other objects on church altars could be made of beautifully worked metal, sometimes ornamented with colored enamel or jewels.

Many English churches belonged to monasteries. A monastery was a place where a group of men or women lived as a community of monks or nuns, devoting themselves to prayer and study. (Today monasteries for women are usually called convents.) Some monasteries, like Westminster Abbey, were on the outskirts or even in the middle of cities. Others were in the countryside or in lonely places such as forests or islands.

Large monasteries frequently owned farms, forests, flocks of sheep, ships, and other property outside the monastery walls. This great wealth not only supported the monks and nuns and allowed them to aid the neighboring poor, but also funded the creation of masterpieces of building, art, and writing.

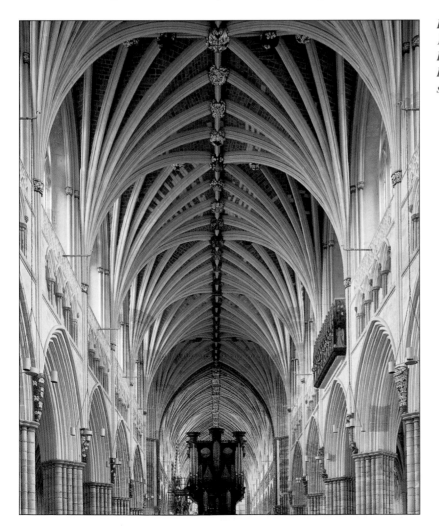

Exeter Cathedral, begun in 1288, is a fine example of English Gothic architecture. Its vaulted ceiling soars sixty-eight feet high.

Wonderful Words

The Britons and Anglo-Saxons both had great traditions of poetry and storytelling. The Christian church had a great tradition of book writing. When these two traditions came together, English literature was born. This literature is among the finest achievements of medieval England.

History and Heroics

The first important work of literature produced in England was actually written in Latin. This was the *Ecclesiastical History of the English People*, by a Northumbrian monk named Bede (ca. 673–735). Because of this book, Bede is often called the Father of English History. He told the story of the Anglo-Saxons, from their arrival in Britain to his own time, in an intelligent, direct, and entertaining style.

Not long after Bede's death, *Beowulf*, the greatest existing early English poem, was composed by an unknown author. In this lengthy work, Beowulf is an idealized Anglo-Saxon warrior: strong, brave, loyal, and generous. He journeys to Denmark to help the Danish king, whose royal hall has been besieged for years by a terrible monster named Grendel. Beowulf then faces and overcomes an even more fearsome monster, Grendel's mother. At last he meets his match, a fire-breathing dragon. Beowulf kills the dragon but receives a death wound in the process. At his funeral he is given the honor and praise that his heroic deeds have earned.

While the poet who composed *Beowulf* looked back on the legendary past, other writers soon began to compile a factual historical record, the *Anglo-Saxon Chronicle*. The chronicle is made up of short yearly entries describing major events. Alfred the Great encouraged the keeping of this record, which was passed around among various important English churches. It is our best source of knowledge about England for the two centuries before the coming of William the Conqueror.

Love Songs, Romances, and Dreams

When the Normans invaded England, so did their language. French became the language of the upper classes. English was used for fewer and fewer writings; the last entry in the *Anglo-Saxon Chronicle* was made in 1154, the year Henry II became king of England. Henry's queen, Eleanor of Aquitaine, was an enthusiastic supporter of the arts, especially poetry

King Arthur and his knights gather at the Round Table in this illustration from a fifteenth-century French manuscript.

and music. At this time, love songs were very popular in southern France, Eleanor's homeland. A common theme in these songs was courtly love, a man's love for a noble lady, who often did not return his love. Nevertheless, the man praised her beauty, sense, courtesy, and other noble qualities, swearing to serve her faithfully all his life. Queen Eleanor probably helped this type of song become popular in England, too. Eventually such poems were written in English as well as in French.

Another kind of French poetry making a strong impression in England was the romance, a long poem about knights, ladies, love, and adventure. One of the first great writers of romance in England was Marie de France, who may have been Henry II's sister. Many of her tales took place at the court of King Arthur. This legendary British hero had become famous all over Europe. Almost everyone enjoyed reading or hearing stories about him and the knights and ladies of his court.

The greatest Arthurian romance in English is *Sir Gawain and the Green Knight*, written by an unknown author during the fourteenth century. In this poem a strange knight dressed all in green brings a bizarre challenge to Arthur's court: He will give his great ax to any knight who is brave enough to strike him with it. Then, one year later, that man must go to the Green Knight and receive an ax-blow from him. Gawain accepts the challenge and beheads the Green Knight—who then picks up his severed head, which reminds Gawain to keep the other half of the bargain. In a year's time, Gawain rides off into the wild forest. After many adventures he finally comes to the Green Knight and submits to the stroke of the ax. But the Green Knight only nicks the back of Gawain's neck, sparing him because of his bravery and sense of honor.

The author of *Sir Gawain and the Green Knight* wrote at least three other poems. One of these, Pearl, is about a man's dream or vision of his dead daughter in heaven. Dream-vision poems like this were among the favorite religious works of the time. William Langland's lengthy poem *Piers Plowman*, about a humble peasant and England's troubles in the years after the Black Death, incorporates nine dream visions. Piers Plowman tried to convince its readers to turn to the simple values of Christian faith and love.

The Father of English Poetry

The fourteenth century was a great time for English literature. The upper classes had returned to speaking English instead of French, and the middle class was growing and becoming better educated. The greatest of all medieval English authors wrote during this time: Geoffrey Chaucer. Born around the year 1340, Chaucer was a middle-class native of London. Along with writing poetry, he worked as a government official and served a term in Parliament. He often read his works aloud to the court of King Richard II.

Some of Chaucer's books, such as *Troilus and Criseyde* (a love story set in ancient times) and *The Legend of Good Women* (about famous women in legend and history), were his own versions of works by the Italian writer Giovanni Boccaccio. *Troilus and Criseyde* is thought by many to be Chaucer's greatest poem. Others believe that *The Canterbury Tales* is Chaucer's masterpiece, and it is certainly his most famous work. It is a collection of twenty-four stories, all in verse, told by a group of pilgrims

A CHOICE FROM CHAUCER

In some of the most famous and influential lines of English poetry, Chaucer's *The Canterbury Tales* begins with this eloquent description of springtime:

> *Whan that Aprille with his shoures sote*
> *The droghte of March hath perced to the rote,*
> *And bathed every veyne in swich licour,*
> *Of which vertu engendred is the flour;*
> *Whan Zephirus eek with his swete breeth*
> *Inspired hath in every holt and heeth*
> *The tendre croppes, and the yonge sonne*
> *Hath in the Ram his halfe cours y-ronne,*
> *And smale fowles maken melodye,*
> *That slepen al the night with open yë,*
> *(So priketh hem nature in hir corages):*
> *Than longen folk to goon on pilgrimages.*

"When April, with its sweet showers, has pierced the dryness of March to the root and bathed every vein in such moisture, and from its power the flower has its beginning; when the West Wind also with his sweet breath has inspired the tender plants in every wood and heath, and the young sun has run half its course through the sign of Aries; and small birds, which sleep all night with open eyes, make melody (as Nature urges them in their hearts): then people long to go on pilgrimages."

A portrait of Geoffrey Chaucer. The poet included himself as a character in The Canterbury Tales, *picturing himself as a simple and overly trusting fellow—but in reality Chaucer was worldly and brilliant.*

who are on their way to visit the shrine of Saint Thomas à Becket in Canterbury. The stories— humorous, serious, religious, and romantic—are typical of the tales that were popular during Chaucer's time. Each story fits the character of the pilgrim who tells it; Chaucer's knight, for example, relates a tale of noble and heroic deeds. Many modern readers find Chaucer's storytellers even more interesting than the stories themselves. Chaucer introduces them all at the beginning of *The Canterbury Tales*, drawing marvelous word pictures of the people of medieval England.

CHAPTER THREE

A CHRISTIAN NATION

When the Anglo-Saxons arrived in Britain, they brought with them their traditional religion, based on the cycles of nature and on the values of their society. They worshipped many deities, including Tiw, god of war; Woden, god of wisdom and kingship; Thunor, god of weather; Frig, goddess of love; and Eostre, goddess of spring. The Anglo-Saxons also believed in nature spirits called elves. We do not know much about how the early English practiced their ancient religion, except that sometimes they made offerings at stones, trees, and springs.

The native Britons, however, were Christian (at least their rulers were; it is difficult to know for certain what the common people believed). This was part of their heritage from the Roman Empire, which had made Christianity its official religion during the fourth century. The empire had stretched from Britain to the Middle East, including most of western Europe and all of southern Europe. Throughout this area the Christian church had become a strong force.

When three-fifths of Britain was taken over by the non-Christian Anglo-Saxons, it was a great loss to the church, which believed it had a duty to bring Christianity to all lands and peoples. In 597 the pope, the church's head, sent a group of missionaries to England. The leader of the group was an Italian monk named Augustine. His eloquent preaching greatly impressed Aethelberht, the king of Kent. Aethelberht allowed Augustine to build a church near Canterbury, the capital of Kent, which became England's main religious center. Augustine and his monks preached Christianity throughout the central and southern Anglo-Saxon kingdoms. In 635 an Irish monk named Aidan began the same process in northern England. Gradually and peacefully, the Anglo-Saxons converted to Christianity.

The Son of God

In the Middle Ages, as now, Christianity was based on faith in one all-

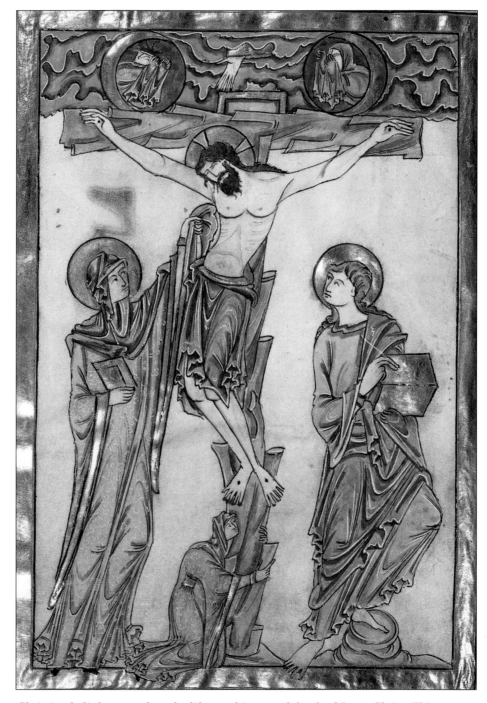

Christian belief centered on the life, teachings, and death of Jesus Christ. This scene of his death is from a book of the Gospels produced in England shortly before the Norman Conquest. At Jesus' side are his mother, Mary, and his disciple John.

powerful, all-knowing God, present everywhere at every time. This same belief was also held by Jews and Muslims. Christianity, however, taught that the one God was revealed as three "persons," distinct from one another yet completely unified. The three-in-one, or Trinity, was made up of God the Father, God the Son, and God the Holy Spirit. The Son was Jesus Christ, and his life and teachings were the centerpoint of Christianity. His story is told in the Gospels, the first four books of the New Testament of the Bible.

Jesus was a Jew who lived in the kingdom of Judea (now Israel) from around 4 B.C.E. to 30 C.E.* The Gospels relate that Jesus was sent by God to save humanity from its sins. His mother was Mary, the wife of a carpenter named Joseph. Before Jesus was born, the angel Gabriel visited Mary to tell her that she would become pregnant with a son who would be great and holy. When it was time for the birth, Mary and Joseph were away from home and had to take shelter in a stable. Angels appeared to shepherds nearby to tell them of the holy infant, and a bright star guided wise men from the East to the birthplace. Shepherds and wise men alike knelt in homage to the newborn baby.

When Jesus was around thirty years old, he went to his cousin John for baptism. This was a ceremony in which John symbolically cleansed people of their past sins so that they could begin to live more righteous lives. For the next three years, Jesus traveled throughout Judea, perform-ing miracles, healing the sick, and teaching. Many of his lessons centered on the power of love—"You shall love your neighbor as yourself" (Matthew 22:39)—and the importance of the Golden Rule—"Whatever you wish that men would do to you, do so to them" (Matthew 7:12). He also taught that those who believed in him and followed his teachings would have an eternal life in the presence of God. Jesus attracted a large number of followers, both women and men. Twelve of these followers, the disciples or apostles, were his most devoted students.

Judea was part of the Roman Empire, and some people feared that Jesus was trying to start a rebellion and make himself king of the Jews. He was arrested and put on trial. Condemned to death by the Romans, he was crucified, or executed by being hung on a cross. Three days later, the

*Many systems of dating have been used by different cultures throughout history. This series of books uses B.C.E. (Before Common Era) and C.E. (Common Era) instead of B.C. (Before Christ) and A.D. (Anno Domini) out of respect for the diversity of the world's peoples.

THE JEWS OF ENGLAND

Although Christianity was the main religion practiced in medieval England, it was not the only one. For a time, the country was also home to a large number of Jews. William the Conqueror encouraged many Jews to move from France to England. Here, as everywhere else in Europe, there were restrictions on the property that Jews could own, the jobs they could hold, and so on. But Jews were allowed to work as traders, merchants, and moneylenders, and English kings and barons came to rely on them financially. For more than a hundred years, English Jews lived and worshipped in peace.

The tide turned in 1189, as Richard I prepared to join the Third Crusade and fight Muslims in the Middle East. Prejudice against all non-Christians was very strong at this time. When a group of Jewish leaders tried to attend Richard's coronation banquet, they were beaten and thrown out of the king's court. This started a riot in London, and many Jews were killed or injured, their goods stolen and their houses burned down. Some Jews were saved from the violence by fleeing to the Tower of London or hiding in the homes of Christian friends.

For the next several months, there were anti-Jewish riots in towns throughout England. The terrible climax came on March 16, 1190, when 150 Jews—men, women, and children—were killed by a mob in the city of York. Describing this time, the historian Ralph of Diceto wrote around 1200, "Throughout England, many of those preparing to join the crusade to Jerusalem decided they would first rise up against the Jews. . . . Wherever Jews were

A scene from medieval European Jewish life: a rabbi, or teacher, instructs a young boy in learning the Hebrew scriptures.

found they were slaughtered by the crusaders, unless the burgesses managed to rescue them. However, let no one believe that wise men rejoiced at the dire and dreadful slaughter of the Jews, for it is written in the Psalms of David which come frequently to our ear, 'Slay them not.'"

Only after the massacre in York did Richard take steps to prevent further outbreaks of such violence. But from this point on, the activities of England's Jews were regulated more than ever. In addition, Jews had to pay huge taxes to the crown; King John taxed them so heavily that many left England altogether. Then, in 1290, Edward I expelled all Jews from his kingdom. For the rest of the Middle Ages, there was no Jewish community in England.

Bible says, some of his women followers went to his tomb and found it empty. An angel told them that Jesus had been resurrected—he had risen from the dead. After this, Jesus appeared several times to his followers, promising forgiveness of sins and resurrection to all who believed in him. Then he ascended to heaven to rejoin God the Father.

Holy Helpers

Like many Christians today, Christians of the Middle Ages honored a large number of saints. The saints were people who had lived exceptionally holy lives and who had the power to perform miracles. God was often felt to be unreachable, so a Christian who needed something might pray to a saint, believing that the saint would then work with God to answer the prayer.

The Mother of God

The best loved of all the saints was Mary, the mother of Jesus. The Bible recorded very little about Mary's life before and after the birth of Jesus. She was present at his first miracle, when he turned water into wine at a wedding. She also visited him at least once while he was preaching, and she stood at the foot of the cross when he was crucified.

Many legends added to Mary's story. One of the most important legends said that when Mary lay dying, the Holy Spirit brought all the disciples to her bedside. Jesus appeared, and she asked him to promise that everyone who prayed to her would receive mercy. Once her request was granted, she died. She was immediately taken up to heaven, body and soul, to reign beside her son.

Many English churches had a special place called a Lady Chapel set aside to honor Mary. Songs were sung in her praise not only in church but also in noble courts. To medieval Christians, Mary was the merciful Mother of God, the Queen of Heaven, and the most perfect human being who had ever lived.

Saints with Special Concerns

People, countries, cities, churches, and organizations of craftspeople usually had one or more patron saints. The patron saint was the special protector and helper of the person or group. Often a patron saint was chosen because

Saint Dunstan, who was archbishop of Canterbury from 960 to 988. Earlier in his life he had been a hermit and had supported himself as a goldsmith. He was especially skilled at making golden objects for use in religious services. A popular story told how the devil frequently tried to tempt Dunstan to stop this holy work. Dunstan finally lost patience, grabbed the devil's nose with red-hot tongs, and made him swear to stop bothering him. Medieval goldsmiths and jewelers regarded Dunstan as their patron saint.

of some similarity between an event in the saint's life and the activities of a particular group. For example, a popular medieval story told of Saint Crispin, a young Roman nobleman who became a Christian. As he traveled from place to place to preach the new religion, he supported himself as a shoemaker. In one town he made shoes for many poor people, refusing any payment for his work. At night angels came and gave him leather to make more shoes for the poor. Because of this, Saint Crispin was regarded as the patron of shoemakers and other leatherworkers.

England's first patron saint was Edward the Confessor. But when King Richard I was crusading in the Middle East, he had a vision of Saint George, who promised him victory in battle. Eventually Saint George was proclaimed the new patron saint of England, and his feast day on April 23 became a national holiday.

Another saint who became very important to the people of medieval England was Thomas à Becket (also known as Saint Thomas of Canterbury). A priest, he was close friends with King Henry II, who made him a high official in the English government. Then, in 1162, Henry gave Becket the nation's most important religious post, making him archbishop of Canterbury. The new archbishop took his responsibilities to the church seriously. Soon he and the king were in bitter conflict. Henry wanted to limit many of the church's powers in England, but Becket insisted on maintaining the church's traditional privileges. In 1170 four of Henry's knights murdered Becket while he was praying in Canterbury cathedral. He was immediately honored as a martyr, a person who had died defending the

THE LEGEND OF SAINT GEORGE

Along with being the patron saint of England, in the Middle Ages Saint George was also looked to as a protector of women and a model of knighthood. According to legend, he was born in Asia Minor during the late third century. He became a high-ranking soldier in the Roman army. Traveling through the Middle East, he came upon a city that was being terrorized by a dragon. The creature had already eaten all of the townspeople's sheep. Now, to keep it from destroying the city and surrounding countryside, the people were forced to give it a maiden to eat every day. When Saint George arrived, the king's beautiful daughter Cleodolinda had been chosen to be offered to the dragon. The soldier found her awaiting her fate at the opening of the beast's cave. With the help of God, Saint George was able to defeat the dragon with only one thrust of his lance. He bound the monster with the princess's long sash, and she led the creature into the city, where George beheaded it before the king and all the people. They were so grateful to be rid of the dragon that they agreed to become Christians, like the brave soldier who had rescued them.

The murder of Thomas à Becket, from a fifteenth-century manuscript.

Christian faith. Soon there were reports of miracles occurring at his tomb in Canterbury, and people began to make pilgrimages there. Three years after Thomas à Becket's death, the pope declared him a saint.

Living the Faith

Ordinary Christians rarely aspired to the great holiness of the saints. In fact, it can be difficult to know how ordinary women and men understood their religion. For one thing, church services were given almost entirely in Latin, the official language of the church. Sometimes a priest would preach a sermon in English, explaining the Bible and the church's teachings in ways that people could understand. Very few could read the Bible for themselves. It was written in Latin—and besides, the average person in medieval England could not read at all.

Medieval preachers often complained that it was difficult to convince the common people to attend church regularly. However, the church was strongly supported by most rulers and nobles, and it played a major role in education and the arts. Christian ideas, values, and symbols were present in nearly every facet of society. Most people in medieval England did consider themselves Christians, even if they may not have understood or lived by all of the church's teachings.

Very religious people attended church frequently to hear Mass. Much of this worship service, held every day, was sung by the priests and choir. The high point of Mass was the sacrament of Holy Communion, which was modeled on the Last Supper, Jesus' final meal with his disciples. He had given them bread and wine, declaring that these were his body and blood, and bid them eat and drink in memory of him. At Communion the priest gave specially blessed wafers, called the Host, to the congregation, saying, "*Hoc est corpus Christi*" ("This is the body of Christ"). Wine was also blessed in the name of Jesus, but only the priests drank it. The church taught that during Communion, Christ was truly present in the Host and the blessed wine.

For the Grace of God

Holy Communion was (and is) one of the church's seven sacraments. The sacraments were rituals or ceremonies that both demonstrated God's grace and bestowed it on those taking part in the sacrament.

Soon after babies were born, they were welcomed into the church by the sacrament of baptism. The child was sprinkled with holy water and blessed in the name of God the Father, the Son, and the Holy Spirit. The parents and godparents pledged to raise the child to live according to the church's teachings. The sacrament of confirmation, in which the child was anointed with holy oil, made the baptism complete. Beginning in the thirteenth century, children received confirmation around the age of seven instead of right after baptism.

In the sacrament of confession or penance, individuals confessed their sins to God through a priest. The priest would assign a penance for the worshipper to perform in order to atone for the sins. Often the penance would take the form of saying a certain number of prayers. Some

A medieval stained-glass window from York shows a wealthy couple kneeling in prayer.

people confessed once a year or more, while others postponed confession until they were dying.

The last sacrament that every Christian expected to go through was extreme unction. A person who was thought to be close to death would make a last confession to a priest. The priest forgave the sins that were confessed and then anointed the person with holy oil in preparation for death.

Most people also took part in the sacrament of matrimony, or marriage. But priests, monks, and nuns were not allowed to marry. The sacrament of holy orders was for men who dedicated their lives to serving the church by joining the priesthood.

CHAPTER FOUR

THE ORDER OF THINGS

In the Middle Ages, very few people believed in any sort of equality. In every relationship, one party was superior to the other. Almost everyone in medieval England had a lord—someone more powerful and of higher social rank, to whom various services were owed.

A noble's lord was either a more powerful noble or the king. The lord granted land and gave protection to the lower-ranking noble, called a vassal. In return, the vassal pledged loyalty and obedience to the lord, particularly promising to fight in the lord's service. This military and political arrangement, which developed in the early Middle Ages, is known as feudalism (FYOO-dull-ih-zum).

History books often used to describe feudalism as the social system of the Middle Ages. It was thought that there was a feudal "chain of command" that stretched from the mightiest king all the way down to the lowliest peasant. More recently, though, historians have shown that feudal relationships affected only the top levels of medieval society—the kings, nobles, and knights.

Peasants were not part of this feudal network. The relationship between peasants and their lords, often called manorialism (muh-NOR-ee-uh-lih-zum), was different. As in feudalism, peasants expected their lord to provide protection and were granted land by him. But instead of military service, peasants gave the lord a portion of their labor and its products or, later in the Middle Ages, made cash payments to the lord. Manorialism was the basic economic system in much of medieval Europe, but it was strongest of all in England.

Worshippers, Warriors, and Workers

The feudal and manorial systems reflected a deeply held belief in divine order. In heaven God ruled over angels and saints, all of whom had their appointed tasks in God's service. Medieval people felt that earthly society

At the top of medieval England's power structure was the king, whose subjects owed him payments and services of many kinds.

was meant to follow the same kind of pattern, the king ruling over nobles and peasants, each group with its specific roles to play. The spiritual concerns of earthly society were looked after by the church, whose head was God's representative on earth, the pope. Beginning in the eleventh century, medieval thinkers tended to divide society into the Three Estates, or classes: those who pray, those who fight, and those who work.

Those Who Pray

Many religious people in the Middle Ages wished to be able to leave the world behind and turn all their thoughts to God. Some of these people, women and men alike, became hermits, while many others joined monasteries. Monks and nuns took vows to spend the rest of their lives in poverty (they were not allowed to own any personal property), chastity (they could not marry), and obedience (to the head of the monastery and to the church's teachings). Monasteries also had rules that covered such details as how monks and nuns should sleep, what they should eat, and what their clothing should be made of. All this was designed to help the monks and nuns think of God and the monastery community before themselves.

Monastery life revolved around a regular schedule of prayer services,

In Anglo-Saxon times a number of religious communities were double monasteries, for both men and women. The monks and nuns lived and worked in separate buildings but shared a church. Anglo-Saxon double monasteries were always governed by a high-ranking nun called an abbess. Some of these women were highly influential, such as Hild of Whitby, shown here in an early twentieth-century illustration. Hild made her monastery a great center of learning and she was so wise that kings and noblemen, as well as ordinary people, sought her advice.

which took up much of the day and part of the night. Between services, monks and nuns were supposed to spend time working and reading. The work could take many forms, including tending the community's beehives or gardens, making candlesticks or clothes, and copying out or illustrating books. When it was time for study, monks and nuns chose their reading from works of philosophy, religious thought, history, and ancient literature.

Beginning in the thirteenth century, there were also groups of monks, called friars, who did not stay in monasteries. The friars traveled from place to place, preaching, teaching, and helping the poor. An additional group of religious people, known as canons and canonesses, lived in monastery-like institutions but spent much of their time doing good works among the common people. Many groups of canons and canonesses ran hospitals and schools.

Another religious path open to men (but not to women) was the priesthood. Priests were empowered to offer Holy Communion, to preach, to bless, and to forgive sins. Some men, known as clerks, completed only part of the training for the priesthood. These clerks might become teachers in schools or universities. Their training also enabled them to take up important positions in government and in noble households.

Like monks, priests were not supposed to marry. However, until the twelfth century it was fairly common for a country priest to have a wife and children. Eventually the church established severe penalties for married priests. Church leaders feared that priests with families would be distracted from giving all of their time and energy to God's service.

Those Who Fight

In England after 1066, all land belonged to the king. A large portion was reserved for his own use, and a great deal was also held by the church. The king granted the use of the rest to his vassals, the barons. In return for these land grants, called fiefs, the barons acknowledged the king as their lord, pledging to fight for him in person and also to provide a certain number of knights in time of war. The barons in turn granted portions of their fiefs to lower-ranking nobles in exchange for military service. These men, too, might take on vassals.

Vassals of all ranks had various nonmilitary duties to their lord, including escorting the lord on his travels, guarding his castles, and always being ready to welcome a visit from him. The lord had the right

Sir Geoffrey Luttrell, a fourteenth-century knight, receives his helmet and shield from his wife and daughter-in-law before riding off to battle.

to summon his vassals to a council at any time. If the lord was taken prisoner in war, his vassals had to pay ransom money to free him. Beginning in the twelfth century, vassals could make a money payment to their lord instead of fighting in his service, and this became a common practice.

Usually when a lord died, his holdings passed to his oldest son. If he had no sons, a daughter could inherit. However, an heir or heiress had to receive the overlord's approval to inherit, had to pay a fee for the privilege, and had to make renewed vows of loyalty. In spite of these vows, vassals often rebelled against their lord. The barons in particular were very protective of their rights. If they believed that the king was limiting their power too much or making too many demands on them, they were usually quick to rise against him.

In addition to his duties to his overlord, a lord had his lands to look after. He also had responsibilities in the justice system. The most serious crimes—treason, making false money, kidnapping, and murder and other violent offenses—were tried only by the king's court. Each lord administered his own court to handle the less serious crimes that occurred on his lands. Convicted criminals were charged fines, which were paid to the lord. In fact, such fines often made up a good portion of a lord's income.

Those Who Work

When medieval thinkers discussed "those who work," they generally meant the people who worked the soil, raising crops and livestock: the peasants. Their work included plowing, planting, weeding, and harvesting the grainfields; and feeding, milking, shearing, and slaughtering animals. Women and older children took part in this work almost as much as men. Women were also responsible for all household work and for most food processing, such as making cheese and butter.

Some peasants worked as blacksmiths, carpenters, shoemakers, weavers, millers, or the like. Often they practiced these trades along with farming. Many women brewed and sold ale, and nearly all women did spinning and sewing. Most cloth making was done for the family, but sometimes women also earned wages for this work.

Before the tenth century, peasants tended to live on isolated farms or in clusters of just a few houses. After this time, and especially in central England, most peasants lived in villages like those described in Chapter Two. Each village was part of a manor, an estate held by a lord. The manor was made up of land under the

English peasants harvesting wheat in the early 1300s. The work is supervised by a reeve, an official of the manor. The reeve was a prosperous peasant who was usually elected to his position by fellow villagers.

lord's direct control and land that he rented to peasant families.

Around the year 1200, peasants were legally categorized as either unfree or free. These categories had to do with how much service they owed to the lord. The unfree were known as serfs or villeins (vih-LANES). They were required to work the lord's land or perform other jobs a certain number of days each week. By the thirteenth century, however, many lords were accepting money instead of work from their serfs.

Serfs also owed the lord numerous fees. There was an annual payment known as head money, which symbolized the serfs' bond to their lord. The lord could demand a tax called tallage whenever he needed extra cash. When an unfree woman married, her family had to pay the lord a fee. When a villein died, the lord was given the family's best cow or sheep. There was still another payment when a serf took over a landholding, whether it was bought or inherited. Villeins also had to turn over farm products at particular times of year—for example, a certain number of chickens and eggs at Easter.

Both free and unfree peasants paid the lord some form of rent for their land. Otherwise, free peasants owed the lord little labor and were exempt from all the fines and fees imposed on villeins. Many records survive of villeins going to court to try to prove that they were actually free; they almost never succeeded. There were other ways, however, to achieve freedom. A serf who moved to a free town and lived there for a year and a day was automatically free. And later in the Middle Ages, lords became increasingly willing to allow serfs to buy their freedom.

A New Society

The concept of the Three Estates described an early medieval model of society. But the second half of the Middle Ages saw the development of a new class of people who did not fit into that model: town dwellers. In 1086 about one-tenth of the English population lived in towns, but by 1300 a fifth of England's people were town dwellers. Some English towns were small, with fewer than five hundred residents. A growing number, however, had populations in the thousands.

At first all English towns were under the lordship of the king, a baron, or a powerful monastery. Many towns, though, wanted to govern themselves. Toward the end of the twelfth century, some cities began to

CHAUCER'S THREE ESTATES

In the prologue to *The Canterbury Tales*, Geoffrey Chaucer described each of the pilgrims traveling to Canterbury. Among his descriptions he included portraits of ideal members of the Three Estates: a knight, a parson (parish priest), and a plowman.

The Knight

A knight there was—and that a worthy man—
That from the time that he first began
To ride to battle, he loved chivalry,
Truth and honor, freedom and courtesy.
Full worthy was he in his lord's war,
And thereto had he ridden, no man so far,
In both Christendom and in heathen places.
He was ever honored for his worthiness. . . .
His bearing was as meek as it could be;
He never spoke rudely or unbecomingly
To anyone in any rank of life.
He was a true, perfect, noble knight.

The Parson

There was a good man of religion,
A poor parson of a small town,
Who Christ's gospel truly preached.
His parishioners he would devoutly teach.
He was good-willed and wondrously diligent,
And in adversity always patient. . . .

His parish was wide, with houses far asunder,
But he never failed, in rain or thunder,
In sickness or in trouble, to visit
The farthest parishioners, well-off or not. . . .
To draw his fold to heaven by fairness
And good example—this was his business. . . .
The teachings of Christ and of the Twelve
Were what he taught—but first he followed
   them himself.

The Plowman

With the parson there was a plowman, his
   brother,
Who had hauled many a cartload of manure.
A good and honest laborer was he,
Living in peace and perfect charity.
He loved God best with his whole heart
At all times, whether life was easy or hard,
And next he loved his neighbor as himself.
He would thresh and also dig and delve,
For Christ's sake, for every poor creature,
Without any pay, if it lay in his power.

A manuscript from around 1460 shows the knight (second from left) and some of Chaucer's other pilgrims leaving Canterbury after their pilgrimage. The cathedral's spire rises above the city wall behind them.

buy charters of freedom from the king. Now, in exchange for a yearly payment to the king, these cities could collect their own tolls, taxes, and court fines. Moreover, the town's leading citizens—the wealthy merchants—were able to elect a mayor and other officials. Elsewhere, lords and towns were often able to reach compromises: the lord might agree to choose the officials who governed on his behalf from among the most prominent townspeople. Some towns had long struggles to obtain any degree of self-government. The citizens of Bury Saint Edmunds, for example, fought their lord for more than a century to win the right to elect town officials.

Taking Care of Business

Town dwellers earned their livings mostly from trade and manufacturing. People who worked at the same craft or trade typically belonged to a guild. Guilds set standards for workmanship, regulated wages and employment practices, paid for members' funerals, and looked after members' interests in other ways.

One of the guild's most important functions was to regulate the training of apprentices, or student craftspeople. An apprentice spent from four to twelve years learning a trade from a master. During this time, the apprentice usually lived in the master's home, and the master supplied the apprentice with food and clothing as well as training. When apprentices finished their training, they had to prove to the guild that they knew their trade and that they were prepared to go into business for themselves. They swore that they were loyal and careful, honest and responsible. Finally, after paying a fee, they were accepted as masters and full members of their guild.

Most townspeople did not have specialized, skilled crafts or trades. Many, especially young women who came from country villages, were servants. Others were vendors, selling items such as bread, eggs, or fruit door-to-door or in the street. Unskilled laborers probably made up the majority of workers in the medieval city. Often they had no regular employment but took whatever jobs were available, day by day.

However they earned their living, most medieval townspeople worked just as hard as country dwellers. For both, the average workday was from ten to fourteen hours long. Unless there was a holiday during the week, Sunday was the only day off.

Women's Rights and Roles

Anglo-Saxon laws and customs recognized women as intelligent, independent beings with many legal rights. But in the eleventh century, two things happened that changed the status of women in England. One was a reform movement in the church, which established new and stricter laws about marriage and women's roles. The other was the Norman Conquest, which brought French laws and customs to England.

According to Norman law, the oldest son inherited all property; a daughter could inherit only if there was no living son. If a man died before his wife, the widow received only a third of his property. Until 1215 a widow who wanted to remain single or to marry a man of her own choosing had to pay a large fine to her lord.

In Norman England an upper-class marriage typically was arranged by the parents, often while the future bride and groom were still children. (Peasants tended to have more choice, since their marriages usually did not involve the transfer of large amounts of land from one family to another.) In the twelfth century, church law did state that both bride and groom had to consent to a marriage for it to be legal. A girl was considered old enough to give her consent at age twelve, a boy at fourteen. A married woman could not make a contract, will, or land sale without her husband's agreement. If a wife did not give birth to any children, a husband could divorce her for that reason alone. Such things had been unheard-of among the Anglo-Saxons.

A Fourth Estate?

To most writers in the second half of the Middle Ages, women had no part in the ideal of the Three Estates. Women were expected "to marry and to serve" those who fought and those who worked. Priests, lawmakers, and other thinkers generally agreed that women were weaker, less intelligent, and more sinful than men. Many laws came to reflect this attitude.

In spite of these disadvantages, women played important roles in society. Since warfare and other dangerous activities were a major part of the lives of medieval noblemen, their death rate was very high. This left many women widowed and many men with no living sons to inherit their lands. Widows and heiresses therefore held fiefs and fulfilled most of the duties of vassals.

A noblewoman who did not hold fiefs of her own still had an impor-

IF YOU LIVED IN MEDIEVAL ENGLAND

If you had been born in medieval England, your way of life would have been determined by the facts of your birth—whether you were a girl or a boy, a noble or a commoner, rich or poor. With this chart you can trace the course your life might have taken as a free peasant.

You were born in a country village. . . .

As a Boy . . .   As a Girl . . .

You live with your family in a cottage on a small plot of land. As a toddler, you have a few wooden toys and also play imaginatively with leaves, flowers, sticks, and everyday objects. Your mother teaches you the most important Christian prayers and beliefs.

As a child you begin to help out on your family's farm. Your first job is probably to scare birds away from newly sown grain, and then you may be put in charge of herding geese or sheep.

As a teenager you continue to work at farming, taking on heavier tasks as you grow stronger. You may also learn a craft—perhaps blacksmithing, carpentry, or leatherworking—from your father or a village craftsman.

As a young man you probably marry, most likely a village girl whom you already know and like. Your family arranges your marriage. You and your wife may live with your parents for a time before you move into a cottage of your own. You rent both your home and your farmland from the lord of the manor.

In your thirties and forties you continue to farm and perhaps to work at a craft. You become a respected man and are elected to important village offices, supervising harvests and the like.

As a child you spend most of your time with your mother, learning how to spin, weave, cook, and sew. You also help look after the family's farm animals.

As a teenager you are old enough to be married. Your family arranges your marriage, probably to a young man whom you already know and like.

As a young woman you have several children, although some of them die while still very young. In addition to making your family's food and clothing, you care for the farm animals, work in the garden and fields, and take farm products to market to sell. You may also earn some extra money by brewing and selling ale or by spinning and weaving.

In your thirties and forties you stop having children. As you age, villagers respect you for your wisdom and experience. In addition to your regular household and farming activities, you may also play an important role as a midwife or healer.

If you become too old to work, you move in with one of your children. Most people do not live much beyond the age of fifty. When you die, your body is buried in the parish churchyard, and the priest says masses for the sake of your soul.

tant position. She assisted her husband in many of his duties, and she was generally in charge of the household. She might supervise the management of the lord's manors and often had responsibility for the family finances. Sometimes she fulfilled her husband's official duties, such as holding court. If her husband was away, a noblewoman might rule his lands—and protect them if necessary—until he returned.

The greatest range of activities open to women at this time was in the towns. Here women practiced almost every trade and craft that men did, supporting themselves and their families. Wives could work at their husband's trade or at an entirely different one. Craftsmen often taught their craft to their wives and daughters as well as their sons, and there were guilds that admitted the widows and daughters of master craftsmen as full members. Some crafts, such as making silk cloth, were completely in women's hands. A few women even became wealthy as merchants. Still, these women had no voice in town government.

For the majority of Englishwomen, who were peasants, life was probably much the same throughout the Middle Ages. They worked in the house, in the farmyard, in the pastures, and in the fields from sunup till sundown. Their work was not as highly valued as men's, yet their contributions to family and community were just as important. These women have been ignored by history for a long time, but today they are finally beginning to receive the attention they deserve.

In a manuscript from the early 1300s a peasant woman performs a common farmyard chore: feeding the chickens.

CHAPTER FIVE

"THERE WILL ALWAYS BE AN ENGLAND"

The culture of medieval England lives on today. Much of its literature continues to be read, its songs sung, and its artworks admired. England has many medieval castles and churches still standing. They attract millions of visitors from around the world, giving tourism a major role in the modern English economy.

Modern England itself is largely a creation of the Middle Ages. The medieval blending of Britons, Anglo-Saxons, Vikings, and Normans created the English nation. Numerous villages and towns founded during the Middle Ages have survived into the present. Modern England's form of government also had its beginnings in the Middle Ages.

In the centuries after the medieval period, England established an empire that included parts of North America, Asia, Africa, and Australia. These areas, too, received much of the heritage of medieval England.

Law and Liberty

In Anglo-Saxon times law and government tended to be local affairs. Even when there was a powerful king, each region of the country was ruled mainly by the area's nobility. The nobles' courts tried all legal cases and made their decisions based mainly on local laws and customs. When the Normans arrived, they took away most of this local authority, putting all power into the king's hands.

Henry II, though following the Norman tradition of strong royal authority, returned much legal power to local courts. However, the courts' decisions now were based on laws that applied throughout England, not

Harlech Castle in North Wales still stands as a monument to medieval English might. The castle was one of many built by Edward I in the late 1200s to secure his control over Wales.

just in the local area. To make sure that the same laws were administered everywhere, Henry sent traveling circuit judges to every part of England. These judges' rulings formed the basis of English common law—legal standards that were held in common by all the English. Centuries later, English common law accompanied settlers to England's overseas

By the 1300s England had three courts of law. The Court of King's Bench dealt with criminal cases (as it still does), the Court of Common Pleas handled civil suits between individuals, and the Court of the Exchequer was responsible for matters related to taxes and government finance. Here the Lord High Treasurer (in red) presides over the Court of the Exchequer, while prisoners (lower left) await a hearing.

colonies, becoming a major influence on the legal systems of the United States, Canada, and many other nations.

The Great Charter

Henry's son John did not have his father's respect for the law. As king, John placed himself above the law, making legal decisions based on his personal wishes. Moreover, he ignored the traditional rights of the barons, his vassals—for example, creating new taxes without consulting them.

In 1214 civil war broke out between the barons and the king. John's army was not strong enough to defeat the barons, and the next year he agreed to meet their terms. On June 15, 1215, the barons presented him with a set of sixty-three articles. Four days later, these articles were written out as a royal charter. It was called Magna Carta, meaning "Great Charter," and copies of it were sent to every part of the kingdom.

Most of Magna Carta's articles were written to guarantee that the king would uphold the barons' traditional rights. It stated, too, that the rights the king granted to his barons were also to be granted by the barons to their vassals. In addition, there were a few articles devoted to the rights of town residents, and one article prohibiting the king from interfering in the affairs of the church. The charter also made an effort to protect Jews and debtors from having their property seized by the king.

Magna Carta established political and legal principles that eventually benefited all English people. It firmly laid down the principle that no one, including a ruler, was above the law. It demanded that law and government be consistent no matter who was in power. Most of all, it upheld individual rights against changeable or tyrannical government. Eventually English colonists carried these legal and political ideals to other lands—including America, where they became part of the foundation of the United States.

Lords and Commons

From Anglo-Saxon times England's rulers were usually advised by a council of nobles and high-ranking churchmen. Magna Carta decreed that this council, which was also the royal law court, always be held at the same place so that people would always be able to seek justice from the king. The Great Charter also required the council to meet together to approve all new taxes. By 1236 this royal council was being referred to as Parliament.

In the mid-1200s King Henry III faced a rebellion by the barons, who demanded more reforms in royal power. The leader of the rebellion was Simon de Montfort. In January 1265 he called a meeting of Parliament, which was as usual attended by the barons and important churchmen. Montfort also summoned, for the first time, leading townsmen and lower-ranking knights from England's shires, or counties. These representatives of the towns and shires became known as the Commons, and they were elected by other members of their class.

King Edward I's Model Parliament of 1295 again included the Commons. By this time Parliament had grown beyond its original role as a royal law court and advisory council. The assembly not only approved taxes but also passed laws and responded to requests for justice from shires, towns, and trade guilds. These expanded functions led to the

King Henry VI with members of Parliament in the 1400s.

Commons being included more and more often, and from 1327 on it was always a part of Parliament. Parliament now had two houses: the House of Lords (made up of the barons and church leaders) and the House of Commons.

Parliament was still less powerful than the king. But as the centuries passed, Parliament came to play an ever-greater role in England's government. Today the English monarch is mainly a ceremonial figure. Parliament, however, continues as the law making body of England—much changed since the Middle Ages, but directly descended from the medieval Parliaments all the same. What is more, England's Parliament provided an important model for the United States Congress, the Canadian Parliament, and many other representative assemblies throughout the world.

Parliament today. A new session of Parliament begins every autumn with the monarch (currently Queen Elizabeth II) coming to the House of Lords at Westminster for the ceremony of the State Opening of Parliament.

Learning and Literature

From Anglo-Saxon times onward, England always had great centers of learning. At first these were monasteries; later, schools grew up around cathedrals and other important churches. Originally organized to educate future priests, in the eleventh century these schools began to take additional students—sons of nobles and well-to-do citizens. The same thing was happening in other parts of Europe, too, especially France and Italy. By the twelfth century, there were many renowned cathedral schools. Each tended to have its own specialties, and students often traveled from school to school over the course of many years. This was the beginning of the European university.

The first university in England developed in the city of Oxford, about fifty miles northwest of London. During the 1100s, there were a number of schools in Oxford, which gradually joined together to form the

All Souls College is one of Oxford University's oldest colleges. It was founded in 1438 by King Henry VI as a memorial to Englishmen who had died in the Hundred Years War.

university. In 1209 students and townspeople in Oxford clashed violently on several occasions. A group of students and professors then moved to the city of Cambridge, founding a new university there. Oxford and Cambridge Universities both continued to grow and thrive. Today they remain among the world's most famous and influential institutions of higher education.

Science Strides Forward

Already in the thirteenth century, Oxford University was producing great scholars. For example, Robert Grosseteste (ca. 1175–1253) was first a student and later a teacher at Oxford. He wrote many works about religion, mathematics, and science. He was especially interested in astronomy and optics, the study of light. He also explored subjects such as the moon's influence on the tides and the way in which the sun produces heat.

Grosseteste's most notable student at Oxford was Roger Bacon (ca. 1214–1292), who became one of medieval Europe's foremost scientists and philosophers. Grosseteste taught Bacon the importance of scientific

Roger Bacon, one of the greatest scientists of the Middle Ages

methods of observation, research, and experimentation. Today Roger Bacon is regarded as one of the founders of experimental science.

Like his teacher, Bacon studied optics. He explained such phenomena as the formation of rainbows and wrote the world's first accurate description of the optic nerve and the anatomy of the eye. He promoted the study of mathematics as a key to scientific knowledge and was interested in other fields, too. After studying ancient Greek scientific ideas—and combining them with his own observations—Bacon concluded that air, like water, has a kind of solidity. He predicted that if someone could build a flying machine in the right way, it would be supported by air just as a ship is supported by water.

Many writers in recent centuries have described the Middle Ages as a time when people were so ignorant that they even believed the world was flat. The careers of Roger Bacon and others like him—who were, in fact, completely convinced the earth was round—prove this view wrong. Today we are finally beginning to appreciate the real vibrancy of medieval knowledge and culture.

Literary Legacies

Among the most dynamic aspects of medieval England's culture was its literature, which has had a lasting influence throughout the English-speaking world. Many medieval stories, often retold in new forms, remain popular today. This is especially true of the legends of King Arthur and his court. Robin Hood, who first appeared in English peasants' rhyming tales in the 1300s, is another ever-popular character.

Geoffrey Chaucer's impact on English literature and language has endured for centuries. The early English poetic tradition depended on heavy accents and alliteration (the repetition of the same consonant sound in two or more neighboring words). By

The young Robin Hood learns archery in this 1917 illustration by American artist N. C. Wyeth. When Robin Hood first appeared as a character in northern English peasants' tales, he was a famous robber and enemy of the king. It took a few centuries for him to become the noble thief, who stole from the rich and gave to the poor, that we know from modern books and films.

Chaucer's time, French and Latin styles had greatly changed the type of poetry written in England. Chaucer combined French and Italian influences with his own mastery of the English language, creating a new form of poetry. He used rhymed pairs of lines, each line having ten syllables that alternated weak and strong stresses. Technically, this is known as the iambic pentameter rhyming couplet; its pattern can be demonstrated:

da-DUM da-DUM da-DUM da-DUM da-DEE,
da-DUM da-DUM da-DUM da-DUM da-BEE.

Chaucer's new style was copied by most of the poets who came after him, becoming the standard form of English poetry until the 1800s. He also had tremendous influence on the future development of the English language. Thanks to Chaucer's importance and popularity, his London-based dialect, or form, of English soon became the standard for the language.

A Language for the World

Medieval England was a melting pot of languages. When the Anglo-Saxons landed in Britain, they found the inhabitants speaking a Celtic tongue, the ancestor of modern Welsh. Many Britons also used Latin, the language of the Roman Empire. Even after Rome pulled out of England, Latin remained the official language of the church. The Anglo-Saxons brought their own tongue, now generally referred to as Old English, which was closely related to German. Then Viking settlers added their language, Old Norse, to the linguistic mix. Finally, William the Conqueror and his followers were French speakers. In addition, the Bible contributed terms from Hebrew and Greek, and growing international trade brought new words from faraway nations.

Even a short, simple English sentence can use words from several languages. For example, in "The students were hungry for dinner," *students* comes from Latin, *hungry* from Old Norse, and *dinner* from French—all words that entered the English language during the Middle Ages. *The*, *were*, and *for* are descended from Old English words, and the sentence's structure follows a form developed in the wake of the Viking invasions of England.

Today English has become a world language. English colonists in the seventeenth through nineteenth centuries took it to the Americas, Australia, Africa, India, and many other places. American businesses, movies, television programs, and the Internet have taken English to even

ENGLISH: FROM OLD TO MODERN

English has seen a lot of changes since the time of the Anglo-Saxons. They used some letters that we do not: æ (ash) stood for the short *a* sound; þ (thorn) and ∂ (eth) were used for the sounds made by *th*. The Anglo-Saxons also used some letter combinations that seem strange to us, such as *hl* and *hw*, and they wrote the *sh* sound with the letters *sc*. And Old English did not use the letters *j*, *k*, *q*, *v*, *x*, or *z*. Nevertheless, a number of English words are just the same today as they were a thousand years ago—for example, *and*, *me*, *him*, *we*, *on*, *bean*, *east*, *leaf*, and *timber*. Many other words have changed very little, such as *benc* (bench), *camb* (comb), *findan* (to find), *riht* (right), *stane* (stone), *sumer* (summer), and *wul* (wool).

Take a Challenge!

In the list below, cover up the Modern English column and then see how many Old English words you can recognize.

Old English	Modern English	Old English	Modern English
æcs	ax	lufianto	love
andswaru	answer	modor	mother
ba∂	bath	nænig	none
cræftiga	crafty	openlice	openly
cyning	king	pleganto	play
dæg	day	rædanto	read
eorthe	earth	sawol	soul
etanto	eat	sceap	sheep
fæder	father	swuster	sister
freond	friend	togædere	together
gærs	grass	þt	that
hlæfdige	lady	ut	out
hunig	honey	wæs	was
hwær	where	wifman	woman
ic	I	ynce	inch

more parts of the world. At least one-tenth of the people on earth use English as their primary language. Millions more use English as a second language, for government, business, education, and communication. In a number of countries, from Sweden to Senegal, schoolchildren are required to learn English, which is more and more regarded as the international language of business and technology. All in all, there are probably close to a billion people today who use the language created in medieval England.

Medieval England: A Time Line

500 C.E.   **700**   **900**

mid-400s
Anglo-Saxons
begin to settle
in Britain

597
Saint Augustine of
Canterbury arrives in
Kent to begin converting
the Anglo-Saxons to
Christianity

731
Bede writes *The
Ecclesiastical
History of the
English People*

871–899
Reign of Alfred the Great

793
First recorded Viking
raid on England

1189–1199
Reign of Richard I
(Richard the Lionheart)

1154–1189
Reign of
Henry II

1534
King Henry
VIII founds the
Church of
England

1100 1300 1500

1016–1035
Reign of
Canute

1042–1066
Reign of Edward
the Confessor

1066
Conquest of England
by William,
duke of Normandy

1086
Domesday
survey

1215
King John signs Magna Carta

1272–1307
Reign of Edward I

1284
Annexation of Wales

1296–1307
Edward I's wars in Scotland

1314
Scots under Robert Bruce defeat Edward II

1315–1317
The Great Famine

1327–1377
Reign of Edward III

1337–1453
Hundred Years War between England and France

ca.1340–1400
Life of Geoffrey Chaucer

1348–1349
Black Death strikes England

1381
Wat Tyler's Rebellion
(English Peasants' Revolt)

1400–1409
Owain Glyn Dŵr's
rebellion in Wales

1413–1422
Reign of Henry V

1455–1487
Wars of the Roses

1476
William Caxton sets
up the first printing
press in England

1485–1509
Reign of Henry VII

1497
Explorer
John Cabot
lands on
northeastern
coast of North
America

GLOSSARY

baron: an English nobleman who held lands directly from the king

bishop: a high-ranking priest who oversees religious affairs for a particular region

cathedral: a church where a bishop has his headquarters. The word comes from cathedra, "throne," because the bishop had his throne, symbolizing his authority, behind the high altar of this church.

cistern: a tank for collecting and storing rainwater

clerk: a scholar studying for the priesthood, or a man who has completed much of the training for the priesthood but has not actually become a priest

dowry: money and/or other property that a woman brings into marriage

fallow: left unplowed and unseeded; land may be left fallow so that it can "rest" and regain its fertility

feudalism (FYOO-dull-ih-zum)**:** a military and political arrangement among kings and noblemen, in which a vassal pledges loyalty and military service to an overlord in return for land and protection

fief: the land that a lord granted to his vassal. Fiefs could also be other property that brought in income, such as mills, toll bridges, and markets.

friar (from Latin frater, "brother")**:** a monk who belonged to one of certain religious societies whose members traveled from place to place, preaching and living off charity

garderobe: an alcove with a kind of toilet seat built over a chute or drainpipe that led to a pit, ditch, or river

guild: an organization of people in the same craft or trade. The guild set standards of training and workmanship and looked after its members' interests in various ways.

knight: a warrior of the noble class, trained to fight on horseback

manor: an estate held by a lord, made up of his own land and land held by peasant villagers in exchange for rents and services

manorialism (muh-NOR-ee-uh-lih-zum): the arrangement between peasants and their lords, in which peasants held land from the lord and owed him various fees and services in exchange

missionary: a person who travels to a far-off place to teach his or her religion to the people of that placemonastery:a place where a group of men or women live as a community of monks or nuns, devoting themselves to prayer, study, and work

penance: actions taken to show sorrow for and make up for sinful behavior

pilgrimage: a journey to an important religious site, for example a church that houses the remains of a saint

saint: a person recognized by the church as being especially holy and able to perform miracles both during life and after death

Scandinavia: the northern European countries of Norway, Sweden, and Denmark

serf: an unfree peasant, with specific financial and labor obligations to an overlord; a villein

vassal: a noble who held land from a king or more powerful noble in exchange for military service and a pledge of loyalty

villein (vih-LANE): an unfree peasant; a serf

FOR FURTHER READING

Chaucer, Geoffrey. *Canterbury Tales*. Selected, translated, and adapted by Barbara Cohen. New York: Lothrop, Lee and Shepard, 1988.

Child, John, et al. *The Crusades*. New York: Peter Bedrick, 1996.

Clare, John D., ed. *Knights in Armor*. San Diego, Harcourt Brace, 1992.

Cosman, Madeleine Pelner. *Medieval Holidays and Festivals: A Calendar of Celebrations*. New York: Charles Scribner's Sons, 1981.

Crossley-Holland, Kevin. *The World of King Arthur and His Court: People, Places, Legend, and Lore*. New York: Dutton, 1999.

Doherty, Paul C. *King Arthur*. New York: Chelsea House, 1987.

Gravett, Christopher. *Castle*. New York: Knopf, 1994.

———.*The World of the Medieval Knight*. New York: Peter Bedrick, 1996.

Hart, Avery, and Paul Mantell. *Knights and Castles: 50 Hands-on Activities to Experience the Middle Ages*. Charlotte, VT: Williamson, 1998.

Hartman, Gertrude. *Medieval Days and Ways*. New York: Macmillan, 1952.

Hastings, Selina. *The Canterbury Tales by Geoffrey Chaucer: A Selection*. New York: Henry Holt, 1988.

Hindley, Judy. *The Time Traveller Book of Knights and Castles*. London: Usborne, 1976.

Hinds, Kathryn. *Life in the Middle Ages: The Castle*. New York: Benchmark Books, 2000.

———. *Life in the Middle Ages: The Church*. New York: Benchmark Books, 2000.

———. *Life in the Middle Ages: The City*. New York: Benchmark Books, 2000.

———. *Life in the Middle Ages: The Countryside*. New York: Benchmark Books, 2000.

———. *The Vikings*. New York: Benchmark Books, 1998.

Howarth, Sarah. *Medieval Places*. Brookfield, CT: Millbrook Press, 1992.

———. *What Do We Know about the Middle Ages?* New York: Peter Bedrick, 1995.

Lace, William W. *The Wars of the Roses*. San Diego: Lucent Books, 1996.

Langley, Andrew. *Medieval Life*. New York: Knopf, 1996.

Lewis, Naomi, trans. *Proud Knight, Fair Lady: The Twelve Lais of Marie de France*. New York: Viking Kestrel, 1989.

Macaulay, David. *Castle*. Boston: Houghton Mifflin, 1977.

Macdonald, Fiona. *First Facts about the Middle Ages*. New York: Peter Bedrick, 1997.

Nardo, Don. *Life on a Medieval Pilgrimage*. San Diego: Lucent Books: 1996.

———. *The Medieval Castle*. San Diego: Lucent Books, 1998.

O'Neal, Michael. *King Arthur: Opposing Viewpoints*. San Diego: Greenhaven Press, 1992.

Osborne, Mary Pope, ed. *Favorite Medieval Tales*. New York: Scholastic Press, 1998.

Platt, Richard. *Stephen Biesty's Cross-sections: Castle*. London: Dorling Kindersley, 1994.

Steele, Philip. *Castles*. New York: Kingfisher, 1995.

ON-LINE INFORMATION*

Annenberg/CPB Project. *Middle Ages: What Was It Really Like to Live in the Middle Ages?* [http://www.learner.org/exhibits/middleages/].

Britain Express. *Medieval England*.
[http://www.britainexpress.com/History/medieval_britain_index.htm].

Britannia Internet Magazine, LLC. *Abbeys and Cathedrals in England and Wales*. [http://www.britannia.com/church/cath.html].

Britannia Internet Magazine, LLC. *British History*.
[http://britannia.com/history/].

Camelot International. *Camelot International Village*.
[http://www.camelotintl.com/village/index.html].

City of York Cancel. *City of York Walls Tour: A Virtual Walk on York's City Walls*. [http://www.york.gov.uk/walls/index.html].

Price, Brian R. *Knighthood, Chivalry, & Tournaments Resource Library*. [http://www.chronique.com/intro.htm].

Stones, Alison. *Images of Medieval Art and Architecture: Medieval Architecture in Britain*.
[http://vrlab.fa.pitt.edu/medart/image/England/maineng.html].

Tompkins, Kenneth. *Wharram Percy: The Lost Medieval Village*.
[http://loki.stockton.edu/~ken/wharram/wharram.htm].

Widdison, Robin, Francis Pritchard, and Michael Aikenhead. *Durham Cathedral & Castle*.
[http://www.dur.ac.uk/~dla0www/c_tour/tour.html].

*Websites change from time to time. For additional on-line information, check with the media specialist at your local library.

BIBLIOGRAPHY

Alsford, Stephen. *Medieval English Towns*.
[http://www.trytel.com/~tristan/towns/towns.html].

Blanchard, Laura, and Carolyn Schriber. *ORB: The Online Reference Book for Medieval Studies*. [http://orb.rhodes.edu].

Burton, Janet. *Monastic and Religious Orders in Britain 1000–1300*. Cambridge: Cambridge University Press, 1994.

Cantor, Norman F. *The Civilization of the Middle Ages*. New York: Harper Perennial, 1994.

Chaucer, Geoffrey. *The Canterbury Tales*. New York: Modern Library, 1994.

Editors of Time-Life Books. *What Life Was Like in the Age of Chivalry: Medieval Europe AD 800–1500*. Alexandria: Time-Life Books, 1997.

Fell, Christine, Cecily Clark, and Elizabeth Williams. *Women in Anglo-Saxon England and the Impact of 1066*. Bloomington: Indiana University Press, 1984.

Gies, Frances, and Joseph Gies. *Cathedral, Forge, and Waterwheel: Technology and Invention in the Middle Ages*. New York: HarperCollins, 1994.

————. *Life in a Medieval Castle*. New York: Harper & Row, 1974.

————. *Life in a Medieval Village*. New York: Harper & Row, 1990.

————. *Women in the Middle Ages*. New York: Barnes & Noble, 1978.

Hallam, Elizabeth, ed. *The Plantagenet Chronicles*. New York: Weidenfeld and Nicolson, 1986.

Halsall, Paul, site designer. *Internet Medieval Sourcebook*. [http://www.fordham.edu/halsall/sbook1.html].

Herlihy, David. *Women, Family, and Society in Medieval Europe: Historical Essays, 1978–1991*. Providence: Berghahn Books, 1995.

Hibbert, Christopher. *Tower of London*. New York: Newsweek, 1971.

Irvine, Martin, and Deborah Everhart. *The Labyrinth: Resources for Medieval Studies*. [http://www.georgetown.edu/labyrinth].

Kelly, Amy. *Eleanor of Aquitaine and the Four Kings*. Cambridge, MA: Harvard University Press, 1950.

Luria, Maxwell S., and Richard L. Hoffman, eds. *Middle English Lyrics*. New York: Norton, 1974.

McCrum, Robert, William Cran, and Robert MacNeil. *The Story of English*. New York: Viking Penguin, 1986.

Mertes, Kate. *The English Noble Household 1250–1600: Good Governance and Politic Rule*. Oxford: Basil Blackwell, 1988.

Metford, J. C. J. *Dictionary of Christian Lore and Legend*. London: Thames and Hudson, 1983.

Riley-Smith, Jonathan, ed. *The Oxford Illustrated History of the Crusades*. Oxford: Oxford University Press, 1995.

Saul, Nigel, ed. *The Oxford Illustrated History of Medieval England*. Oxford: Oxford University Press, 1997.

Shahar, Shulamith. *Childhood in the Middle Ages*. Translated by Chaya Galai. London: Routledge, 1990.

————. *The Fourth Estate: A History of Women in the Middle Ages*. Translated by Chaya Galai. London: Methuen, 1983.

Tolkien, J. R. R., trans. *Sir Gawain and the Green Knight, Pearl, Sir Orfeo*. Boston: Houghton Mifflin, 1975.

INDEX

Page numbers for illustrations are in boldface

ABOUT THE AUTHOR

Kathryn Hinds grew up near Rochester, New York. In college she studied music and writing, and went on to do graduate work in comparative literature and medieval studies at the City University of New York. She has written a number of books for young people, including Marshall Cavendish's Life in the Middle Ages series and several other Cultures of the Past titles. Kathryn now lives in Georgia's Blue Ridge Mountains with her husband, their son, three cats, and three dogs. She works as Information Specialist at her local public library and in her spare time enjoys music, dancing, reading, and taking long walks in the woods.